Being in Harmony with

Nature

A Collection of Poetry

By
Christopher Viau

Illustrated by
Christopher Viau

In memory of my Grandma
She loved nature. She loved to walk in the woods,
and look at all of natures' beauty.

Table of Contents

Walking Through the Woods

The Old Oak Tree

I am sitting by the old oak tree thinking what this
tree has seen over the years.
Has the tree seen worse weather then I have?
Is it home to birds? What kind of birds?
How many branches did the tree lose over the years?
How old is the tree?
I want say thanks for giving me shade on a hot
summer day.

A Little White Tree

You stand out in the woods.
You bark is white.
Your leaves are round.
Do the birds know you as a tree?
Does one bird love to sit on your braches?

Weeping Willow

Why are you so sad?
You let your   branches hang down almost to the
ground.
You are tall but your branches cover your trunk.
Your green leaves look nice.

Evergreen

You are one of a kind
You live in the coldest places on the planet.
You have not leaves but needles.
They never fall off you in the winter.

Water Ways

The Mighty Power of Rivers

All rivers have a starting point.
All rivers have an ending point.
Some rivers are big for barges to move things like
grains and coal.
While other rivers are small; people can catch fish
along their shorelines.
Rivers are home to fish, animals, and plants.

A Pond in a Nature Park by my House

Fish, frogs and turtles live in the pond.
On the north side there are cottonwood trees, sea-
weed and water lilies.
On the south side there are oak trees and white birch
trees, home to all kinds of birds and animals.
At dusk deer drink from the pond.
The ducks come for their daily swim.
Fishermen cast their lines hoping to catch the
grandpa bass.
Kids skip rocks on the shoreline, and on hot days
they take a dip in the lake.

Sunset on the Lake

On my boat I lay back looking on the day.
The small waves rock my boat back and forth.
The sun hits the water just the right way to make the
water look golden.
The sky turns pink and orange when the sun starts
going down.
The world is peaceful while I am on this boat.

The Frozen Pond

In the middle of winter the pond is frozen over.
Alot of kids like to iceskate on it.
The boys play hockey.
It is like back in the good old days when everyone
knew everyone.
At night fresh new snow fell, you will see animal
tracks.

The Peaceful Gardens

The Midwest Trusted Flowers

Marigolds are orange, red, and yellow.
Marigolds look good from spring through fall.
Marigolds thrive in the sun, but if they are planted in
the shade they will grow, also.
In the middle of summer heat and dry weather.
Marigolds will stay green while grass turns brown.
A lot of water will not drown them.
Marigolds are easy to maintain.

Bush with Enormous flowers

Lilacs can grow up to five feet tall and the bush has huge pink flowers.
You can smell the strong and sweet flowers just walking by the bush.
Some people cut off flowers so they can bring that smell inside.
The bush lasts the whole summer along.
The bush attracts bees to get the pollination from the flowers.

A Valley of Lily

How beautiful it is to look down from a bridge, and
see a large number of lilies in the woods.
You could see little white flowers all over.
The flowers smell amazing.
With a few lilies in a couple of years, they will fill
up a field.

A   Garden with a Lot of Tulips

Tulips are a lot of different colors, and when you look inside, a tulip might have different colored lines inside of them.
The flower brings color to people's yards.
They are bulbs so they come up every year.
Some gardeners use tulips as a borders for their garden, while others gardeners place them around their trees and bushes.
Tulips are one of the first flowers of spring.
In the fall when the tulips come up, you know that winter is just around the corner.

Birds that Control the Sky

Tap on the Window

Early in the morning I heard a tapping noise.
Was it coming from my bedroom or the next
apartment?
Tap, tap, tap, and tap
I thought I was hearing things.
When I was getting dressed, I saw a bird.
I guess he wanted to say good morning.

A V Shape in the Sky

Is this a space ship from another planet?
It sounds like a lot of clucking.
About 20 geese landed like a dance.
They eat worms from the field, before heading south
for the winter.

Sparrows too Many to Count

On a spring morning there are sparrows in a field
looking for worms.
They are searching for twigs and things to build
their nests.
Sparrows fly solo not in a v shape.
In June sparrows' babies come out, and they are so
small.
I wonder how the baby sparrows can fly with such
small wings.

Snow Birds

In the middle of winter, and everything is frozen.
A foot of snow can cover everything.
There is a little red bird that flies around and sits on
a snow covered branch.
How do you stay warm in this bitter cold weather?
Why don't you fly south for winter like a lot of
other birds?

Animals are Around

My Little Squirrel Friend

You live outside of my window jumping from tree
branch to tree branch.
You chase a woman squirrel for fun.
You lie on the tree branch next to my window,
watching American Pickers on my TV.
In fall you start collecting nuts for the long winter
ahead.
In the winter you find the warmest spot to hangout.

At Sunset

In a field at sunset you will find some big animals
feeding on grass.
Deer are light brown and large.
The male deer have antlers.
Their fawns have white spots, and walk with their
mothers.
You can watch deer eating up close.
I am amazed at how close; I could watch deer in a
field.

What is in my Blueberry Bushes?

I planted blueberry bushes along the border of my
yard, next to the woods.
One early morning I was looking out my kitchen
window, when I saw leaves on the blueberry bush
beginning to move.
I saw the bush shake with such force the blueberries
fell off plus some of the leaves.
I saw a bear back by my bushes.
I opened the side door and rang the bell by my door,
and the bear ran off.

Alley Cats

They are homeless.
They have to hunt for food.
They sleep in dirty places like sheds.
They are not clean.
People use things like brooms to get the cats off their land.
A few people use weed killer to poison the cats.
If an animal officer catches them they bring them to the pound, their fate has to come; they will be adopted to love a family or ….

People and Nature

Balancing Act

Can man and nature thrive together?
I look at Chicago and how the skyscrapers are in the
sky line.
The industrial park and coal power plants,
How nature thrives in the city?
Chicago has lakefront for nature and nice parks.
People have rooftop gardens, and some buildings
plant plants on their roofs to keep their buildings
cool.

While I Walked on a Nature Path

I saw pop cans and chip bags on the ground a few
feet from a trash can.
I saw plastic bags all over.
Some people had a picnic but they did not clean up.
Cigarette butts all over on side of the path.
On the path I saw a broken Old Style beer bottle.
Don't people care about nature?
If so, why don't people clean up after themselves?

My Little Green Friends have Gone Away

I live across the street from beautiful woods, where
there is a pond for frogs and other animals.
A year ago, I noticed something was not right; the
workers came with their chain saws.
They cut down all the trees in sight.
My friends hopped around the construction site.
They kept five acres of land with the pond that my
little green friends and all other animals went.
The construction crew finished the last townhouses
two months ago.
Today I heard a pump draining the pond, and I saw a
bobcat removing the land.
The Bobcat picked up the dirt and dumped it into a
dump truck.
Now I live across the street from the new strip mall
with a Pet Go that sells frogs but they have
destroyed a natural habitat.
I am wondering, where my little green friends went.

How Could People Turn away from the Fact?

We are not recycling our plastic, paper, and cans?
If the landfills   fill up where will our trash go?
Why do people use cars that use a lot of gas?
All carbon in air affects the ozone layer.
Trees play big part keeping the air clean.
If we cut down rain forest for our use, can we grow
trees faster to keep up our need?
When we build homes to span our cities how does it
affect nature?
People see or are attacked by wild animals in their
back yard.
We are getting a larger amount of people in the
world, can we handle the population?
It will be a hard for the farmers to keep up with
feeding all of us.

I am Chris Viau. I have Cerebral Palsy. I enjoy writing poems and being in nature. This is my second book that I wrote on nature. The first book I wrote was called Chicago's Seasons. I am an artist at The Arts of Life in Glenview IL. The illustrations in this book, I painted using water colors. I hope you enjoy this book.

41035893R00027

Made in the USA
Charleston, SC
17 April 2015